Ben Biggins' house

by Judith Nicholls

Illustrated by Joan Hickson

This is the tree.

3

This is the tree
that gave the wood.

This is the tree
that gave the wood
that made the door.

This is the tree
that gave the wood
that made the door
that opens wide.

This is the tree
that gave the wood
that made the door
that opens wide
and leads to the hall.

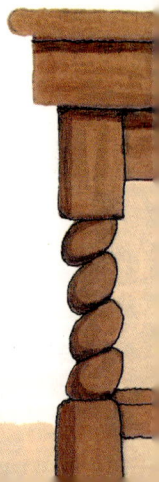

This is the tree
that gave the wood
that made the door
that opens wide
and leads to the hall
where it's warm inside.

Ben

Ben Biggins

13

This is the tree
that gave the wood
that made the door
that opens wide
and leads to the hall
where it's warm inside
by the crooked wall.

14

This is the tree
that gave the wood
that made the door
that opens wide
and leads to the hall
where it's warm inside
by the crooked wall
that holds up the roof.

Jamila

Ben

This is the tree
that gave the wood
that made the door
that opens wide
and leads to the hall
where it's warm inside
by the crooked wall
that holds up the roof
that shelters us all.

This is the tree
that gave the wood
that made the door
that opens wide
and leads to the hall
where it's warm inside
by the crooked wall
that holds up the roof
that shelters us all
in...

MY HOUSE!